MONEY BASICS

PAYING FOR COLLEGE

by Tammy Gagne

BrightP◆int Press

San Diego, CA

BrightP◆int Press

© 2020 BrightPoint Press
an imprint of ReferencePoint Press, Inc.
Printed in the United States

For more information, contact:
BrightPoint Press
PO Box 27779
San Diego, CA 92198
www.BrightPointPress.com

LIBRARY OF CONGRESS CATALOGING-IN-PUBLICATION DATA

Names: Gagne, Tammy, author.
Title: Paying for college / by Tammy Gagne.
Description: San Diego, CA : ReferencePoint Press, 2020. | Series: Money basics | Includes
    bibliographical references and index. | Audience: Grades 10-12
Identifiers: LCCN 2019034002 (print) | LCCN 2019034003 (eBook) | ISBN 9781682828052
    (hardcover) | ISBN 9781682828069 (eBook)
Subjects: LCSH: College costs--United States--Juvenile literature. | Student aid--United
    States--Juvenile literature.
Classification: LCC LB2342 .G328 2020 (print) | LCC LB2342 (eBook) | DDC 378.106--dc23
LC record available at https://lccn.loc.gov/2019034002
LC eBook record available at https://lccn.loc.gov/2019034003

INTRODUCTION   **4**
HOW WILL I PAY FOR COLLEGE?

CHAPTER ONE   **10**
WHY PLAN FOR COLLEGE EXPENSES?

CHAPTER TWO   **24**
HOW DO SCHOLARSHIPS WORK?

CHAPTER THREE   **38**
HOW DO GRANTS AND LOANS WORK?

CHAPTER FOUR   **54**
HOW CAN STUDENTS PAY FOR COLLEGE
OUT OF POCKET?

Worksheet   72
Glossary   74
Source Notes   75
For Further Research   76
Index   78
Image Credits   79
About the Author   80

HOW WILL I PAY FOR COLLEGE?

Emily had waited for this email for weeks. She had applied to five schools. Her guidance counselor called two of them her safety schools. They were the universities Emily had the best chance of getting into. Two were her target schools. She had a good chance of getting into those schools as well. The last was

Getting into college is exciting. But many students worry about how they will pay for it.

her reach school. This was the university

Emily had dreamed of attending since she

was little. But getting into it would be a

challenge. The email was from this school.

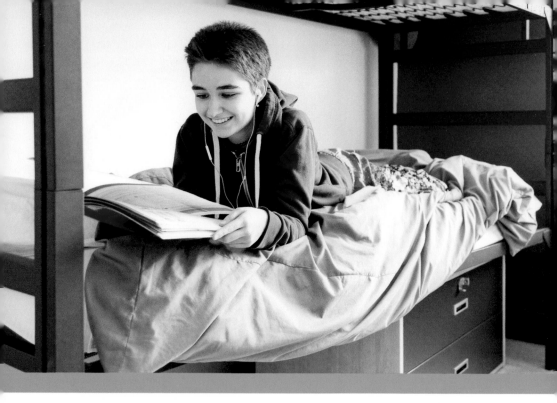

The cost of college is more than just tuition. Students may also have to pay for housing, food, and school supplies.

"Are you going to open it?" her friend Jake asked. He watched Emily stare at her smartphone. She was as still as a statue.

Emily held her breath and tapped the message. She read the first few words: "We are pleased to inform you . . ."

She had gotten in! But she felt sick as she finished reading her acceptance. The school was giving her a **scholarship**. But it would cover less than half the **tuition**. She needed thousands of dollars to save her spot.

"What am I going to do?" she asked Jake. "My parents don't have this kind of money."

"You filled out the FAFSA, right?" he replied. He was referring to the Free Application for Federal Student Aid. "You can probably get the money you need through student aid. I qualified for

There are many ways to pay for college.

some grants. But I'm also taking out

some loans." Jake had received early

admission to his top choice months ago.

Emily remembered filling out the FAFSA

with her parents last fall. She couldn't

remember what she qualified for, though.

She just knew it was enough for her

target schools.

"Don't worry," Jake told her. "I've learned a lot about paying for college. I can help you figure it out, if you would like. Just call me after you talk to your parents. And congratulations! Remember, this is good news."

"You're right," Emily said. "And thanks. I have a feeling I'll be asking you more about this soon."

"I should be the one asking *you* questions," he replied. "You're going to a great school!"

"I am!" she said. She could hardly believe it was really happening.

CHAPTER ONE

WHY PLAN FOR COLLEGE EXPENSES?

Many high school graduates go to college. Going to college can be the first step toward a career. It can also be an expensive step. Students may attend a local community college. They may attend a four-year university far away. No matter what, they will pay tuition.

Columbia University's tuition was $59,430 for the 2018–2019 school year.

THE COST OF COLLEGE

High-status private universities cost the

most. These include schools such as

Columbia University, Duke University, and

Tufts University. Tuition for one year can be

Parents may begin saving for their child's college education when the child is still very young.

more than $50,000. Even public schools carry a big price tag. Students must have a plan for this large expense.

The cost of college has increased over time. The average cost of a four-year degree in 1989 was $26,902. By 2016, the cost was $104,480. The costs of other things have also gone up. This is called inflation. Wages have also increased. But college costs have increased almost eight times faster than wages have. Even after adjusting for inflation, the cost of college still doubled in twenty-seven years.

Many kids in the 1980s didn't think about college costs until high school. Some waited until they were juniors or seniors. Today, many parents start saving for college early. Some start before their kids are even born. The cost of college can lead to high debt. Student loans make up more debt in the United States than credit cards and auto loans combined. Personal finance expert Dave Ramsey addresses this issue on his website. "At this rate," he writes, "college graduates will be lucky to have their student loans paid off before *their* kids start college!"[1]

WAYS TO PAY FOR COLLEGE

There are many ways to pay for college. Opening a college savings account is one way. This account helps pay out-of-pocket costs. Parents, students, and others can contribute money. The money then grows

How the Average Student Pays for College

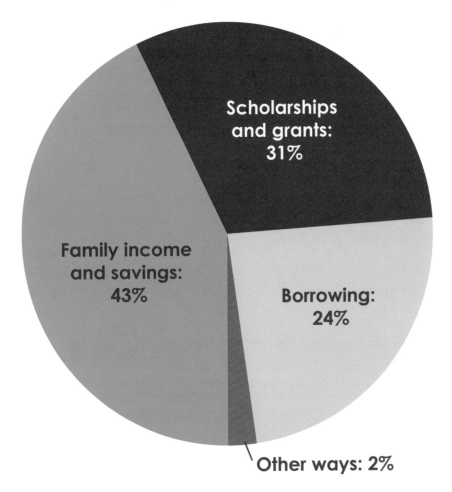

Scholarships and grants: 31%

Family income and savings: 43%

Borrowing: 24%

Other ways: 2%

"How America Pays for College 2019," Sallie Mae, 2019. *www.salliemae.com.*

The average college student in the United States uses a variety of methods to pay for college. Most parents contribute at least some money to their kids' education expenses. The chart above is a breakdown of how the average student pays for college.

over time. The account holder doesn't have to pay taxes on it. As kids get older, they may choose to work part-time to add to their college savings.

Not everyone starts saving from a young age. There are other ways to pay. One is by doing well in classes, sports, and other activities. Students who earn good grades

SIGNING UP

Some students pay for college by joining the military. Students do not need to join full time. They can sign up for the reserves. The US military has this part-time program. Students can also earn money for school through the Army and Air National Guards.

may receive scholarships. This means the school pays for part or all of the tuition. Skilled athletes can earn money for school this way. Students involved in the arts and many other activities can earn scholarships too. Some scholarships require an essay. Others only ask applicants to fill out a form.

Students may also apply for grants. Grants work like scholarships. Neither needs to be paid back. The exception is if the student withdraws from school early. Most grants are based on financial need. Students may not qualify for a grant if their

Students work hard in school to qualify for scholarships.

parents make more than a certain amount of money.

Students should apply for as many scholarships and grants as possible. But these likely won't cover everything. About 20 million students attended college in the fall of 2018. Only 20,000 received full-ride scholarships. These are scholarships that cover all college costs.

Some schools offer work-study programs for students. These let students earn money by working while going to college. The money helps pay their remaining tuition. Some of these jobs are based in community service. Others place the students at low levels in the fields they are studying.

The last option for college students is borrowing money. Student loans can come from the government. They can also come from private companies. Students will have to pay this money back. They will also pay interest. Interest is extra money that borrowers must pay to the lenders.

Student loan debt can add up quickly. It can take many years to pay off. Borrowers with large student loans may get turned down for other loans. Buying a

Parents and students should communicate about how to pay for college.

house could be out of reach. For these reasons, students should use as few loans as possible.

GETTING STARTED

Many parents think they cannot save enough to pay for college. This is often the case for families with several children. But every dollar saved helps. This is true even for students in high school. Kathryn Flynn is a personal finance writer. She says, "Even if your child is in high school there is still time to . . . reduce the amount they will have to borrow in student loans."[2]

HONEST TALK ABOUT COSTS

It is important to know how much parents can contribute to college. Students should not assume that their parents will pay. Parents have their own bills. An honest discussion can help avoid a misunderstanding. Students can ask if they have a college savings account. If not, they may ask their parents to help them open one.

The biggest mistake in saving is not starting. Students need to know how much they can afford. Not saving at all can seriously limit a student's choices. Students could end up being disappointed. They could be accepted to their dream school. But they might not be able to afford it.

CHAPTER TWO

HOW DO SCHOLARSHIPS WORK?

Thousands of scholarships are available to students. Many people think they are for high school seniors only. This is not true. Scholarships are also available for all high school students. Some are available for students already in college. Students shouldn't assume that they are too young

School librarians can help students find scholarships to apply for.

or too old. It can simply take some time and

effort to search.

HOW TO FIND SCHOLARSHIPS

Students can research scholarships

at school or a city library. Guidance

counselors and teachers can offer advice.

Librarians often have experience from helping other students. Several companies publish books of scholarship listings. A new version is published every year. Students can also find books about applying for scholarships. For example, they can find books about writing scholarship essays. A good essay can help an applicant

REACH OUT FOR HELP

Don't be afraid to ask for help when searching for scholarships. Parents, teachers, and other adults can help. Many of these people have gone through the process themselves. Adults can also be wonderful proofreaders for essays. When more people look over an application, there is a better chance of catching mistakes before it gets sent out.

stand out. There can be a lot of competition for scholarships. Every advantage counts.

People can also search for scholarships online. Many websites offer listings of scholarships. They give detailed descriptions and application guidelines. Students can search for scholarships using many criteria. They can look for scholarships for a certain gender. They can search by what they will study. Online databases have information on thousands of scholarships. Some require an account. The site will send students scholarships they can apply for.

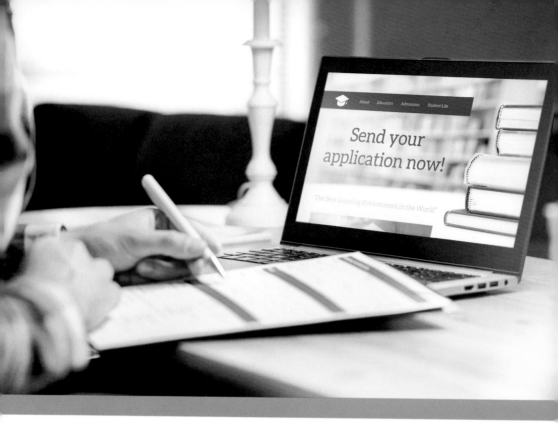

It is important to apply for many scholarships, including small ones.

HOW TO APPLY FOR SCHOLARSHIPS

Journalist Greg Daugherty recommends

taking time to search for scholarships. He

writes, "Treat it like a part-time job and set

aside several hours every month to look

for and apply for scholarships. You should

continue applying for scholarships for as long as you're in school."[3]

There is no limit to how many scholarships a student can get. Students can apply for a variety. They can use each one they receive. Some scholarships are based on merit. This means that they are awarded to students who are high achievers. This can be for academics. It can also be for other activities. Other scholarships are not merit based. This means that they have no achievement requirements. They may have other requirements. For example, some scholarships are specific to a college. Others might be only for students studying physics.

Applying for scholarships can become overwhelming. Students can start by keeping track of application deadlines.

IT'S ALWAYS SCHOLARSHIP TIME

Many people think there is a specific time to apply for scholarships. Many deadlines fall between September and May. But there is no single scholarship season. Students should spend time searching for scholarships all year long. Each one will have its own deadline. Students may even find less competition for scholarships with deadlines outside the norm. Fewer people are applying at these times.

Students should also keep a record of which scholarships they apply for. A good way to do this is by saving a copy of each application. Students should note the date when recipients will be notified. Some students even use a spreadsheet to track this information. They list each scholarship they apply for. They list the notification date. Then they can record each response they receive.

MOST COMMON TYPES OF SCHOLARSHIPS

Scholarships come from many places. The federal government, colleges, and

Some colleges give automatic scholarships based on test scores.

universities provide some. Nonprofit

organizations and businesses can also

provide them. Even families or individuals

can create scholarships.

Students can earn academic

scholarships through their good grades.

Each academic scholarship works differently. Most use a minimum grade point average (GPA). They might also use an ACT or SAT score. Some scholarships are for students with specific **majors**. There are academic scholarships available in the arts and in **vocational** subjects. Academic scholarships are usually guaranteed for four years of college. This means that students will continue to receive the money each year. They just have to maintain a certain GPA.

Athletic scholarships are also available. These are for students who excel in high

The best high school athletes can receive athletic scholarships.

school sports. They are based on past

performance and future expectations.

Scouts look for high school players.

They find players who would contribute

the most to college teams. Most athletic

scholarships are only guaranteed for one

year of school. Student athletes can lose their scholarships for many reasons. These include injuries, poor performance in the sport, or poor grades. Athletic scholarships are not easy to get. Only the very best players receive them. Experts say, "The odds of landing a college scholarship in many major sports are lower than the chances of being admitted to Harvard, Yale, Princeton, or Stanford."[4]

Other scholarships are created for certain groups of people. Some scholarships are exclusively for women. Some are for specific minority groups. Others are open

Students should apply for college scholarships every year they are in high school and college.

to people who are first-generation college

students. This means they are the first

in their families to go to college. These

scholarships often help increase **diversity**

on college campuses. This increases

diversity in the workplace after college too.

Application processes can be as varied

as the scholarships themselves. Following

the individual guidelines is important. Read and follow all the instructions. Answer questions thoroughly. Use good handwriting on forms. Type all cover letters and essays. Read them carefully and fix any mistakes. Most importantly, submit the application before its deadline.

Not all scholarships require lengthy essays. Some do not ask students to write an essay at all. Students who find writing challenging should not rule out scholarships that require essays. Sometimes just a few hundred words can lead to thousands of dollars in tuition.

CHAPTER THREE

HOW DO GRANTS AND LOANS WORK?

Many grants and loans come from the government. To apply, students must fill out the FAFSA. This name stands for Free Application for Federal Student Aid. All high school seniors should fill out this form. They should do this regardless of their families' income.

The US Department of Education awards more than $120 billion a year in student aid.

The FAFSA is the first step for applying for all federal aid.

HOW TO FILL OUT THE FAFSA

The FAFSA is available online. The deadlines are the same each year. The new form comes out on October 1. The deadline

The FAFSA uses both student and parent information.

is the following June 30. Students should

complete this form as soon as possible.

Grant money is limited. It is given first come,

first served. Students who wait too long

may miss out. Students must fill out a new

FAFSA each year. This is the only way to continue their federal aid.

Students and parents will need to create a Federal Student Aid (FSA) ID. The FSA ID is a username and password. It lets people access their financial aid information. It is also an electronic signature.

The FAFSA requires information about parents' finances. It is easiest for parents and students to fill it out together. Parents should have their income tax returns from the year before. Parents will need W-2 forms. They will need bank and investment statements. They will also need mortgage information. Self-employed parents may need to provide additional paperwork. Students with jobs must also provide their income information. Copies of all paperwork submitted through the FAFSA should be printed out and saved. Documents may need to be sent again.

HOW THE FAFSA WORKS

Government workers review the FAFSA. Then applicants receive a student aid report (SAR). The SAR tells students what aid they qualify for. It also lists students' answers to the FAFSA questions. There is another important piece of information on the SAR.

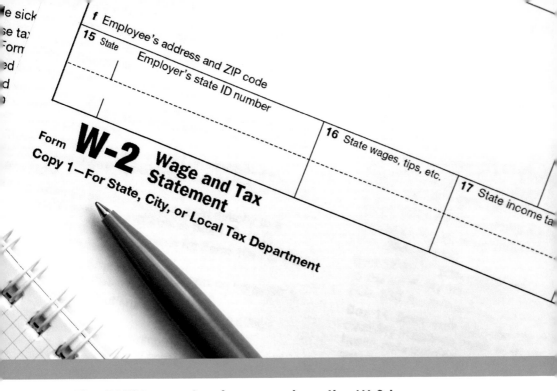

The FAFSA uses tax forms such as the W-2 to see how much income the family has.

It is the expected family contribution (EFC).

This estimates what families can pay for

college. Colleges use the EFC. It helps

them decide how much aid a student

may receive.

A student applies for admission to a

college. That school gets access to the

family's FAFSA. The school breaks down the options for paying tuition. It compares its cost of attendance to the available financial aid.

THE CSS PROFILE

Another important form is the College Scholarship Service (CSS) Profile. This form is different from the FAFSA. The FAFSA is for federal aid. But the CSS Profile is for institutional aid. This means grants from the college. Not every school requires it. But many private colleges do. Around 300 of them require this form. One expert says, "Many schools are sticklers about it.

Around 300 colleges and universities, including Stanford, require the CSS Profile.

If you don't submit it on time, they deny you institutional funding."[5] This form has a twenty-five-dollar fee. That covers sending it to one school. It costs sixteen dollars to send it to each additional school.

WHEN LOANS ARE NEEDED

What happens if scholarships and grants aren't enough? This is where student loans come in. Borrowing money for college is a big commitment. Students can spend many years paying off their debt. Finding a loan with the best terms can make borrowing more affordable.

Students must pay back the money they borrow, plus interest. Interest is charged as a percentage of the unpaid amount of the money borrowed. For government loans, the interest rate is fixed. This means that it stays the same for the length of the loan.

Private loans can come from banks or other

lenders. Some have fixed rates. Others have

variable rates. Variable rates can change

based on the **economy**. They can be

expensive if rates go up. But they can help

if rates go down. Interest rates can make

STUDENT LOANS AND BANKRUPTCY

Bankruptcy is a legal process. It occurs when people have more debt than they can pay. It removes the borrower's responsibility to pay the debt. For example, people may eliminate large amounts of credit card debt in bankruptcy. Student loans are an exception. In most cases, they cannot be **discharged** in bankruptcy. Exceptions can be made in situations of extreme financial and living problems. But proving this can be difficult.

Students may need an adult with good credit to cosign their private student loan.

a huge difference in how much money the student pays over time.

Private loans can have lower interest rates than government loans. But the best rates only go to borrowers with excellent credit. Credit is the ability to borrow money and pay it back later. People who make payments on time have good credit. Late payments cause bad credit. So does high debt. Building good credit takes time. Most students have not built enough for a private loan. Parents can help by cosigning a loan. But cosigning is a big responsibility. If a student does not make payments on time, it hurts the cosigner's credit.

PAYING BACK STUDENT LOANS

It is important to know the loan payment schedule. Borrowers should know how much they will pay. They must know when payments are due. Borrowers must

Most students do not have to begin paying off their student loans until after they graduate.

also know when payments begin. Most

student loans do not require payments

until after graduation. Students can then

focus on studying instead of working.

Additionally, most government loans have

a grace period. This is a six-month period

after graduation. During the grace period, borrowers do not have to pay. They have a chance to find a job and earn money before payments are due.

Elizabeth Aldrich is a finance writer. She explains, "Federal student loans also offer a variety of repayment plans, including an income-driven repayment plan for people who cannot afford high monthly payments."[6] Income-driven plans adjust the payment amount. Payments are capped at a certain percentage of income. Some people might have a minimum payment of zero. But interest will still grow. Students should read the fine print of loan agreements. They must make sure a plan is right for them.

The government will forgive some student loans. This means the borrower doesn't have to pay back all the money. Forgiveness programs are available for people who work in certain fields. These fields include education, health care, and public service. People in these fields must meet certain requirements to qualify for loan forgiveness.

Government loans offer many advantages over private loans. One exception relates to refinancing. This is when a borrower takes out a new loan with better terms. The new loan pays off the old loan. Refinancing usually provides a better interest rate. It can also give more time to pay the money back. The government will not refinance student loans. But students can take out private loans to refinance government loans.

CAN FORGIVENESS PROGRAMS HELP?

Some forgiveness programs create new financial burdens. Some income-driven programs forgive the debt after a certain amount of time. But the government then calls the forgiven debt income. This means that the borrower has to pay taxes on it. If the loan is large, these taxes might be unaffordable.

CHAPTER FOUR

HOW CAN STUDENTS PAY FOR COLLEGE OUT OF POCKET?

One of the smartest ways to prepare for college expenses is saving money. It is ideal to begin setting money aside early. This gives money as much time to grow as possible. Not everyone already has a savings plan. But any amount of

People may spend many years saving for college.

savings can help. Anyone can benefit from saving today.

HOW TO SAVE FOR COLLEGE

There are several ways to save money for college. Many people begin with a simple savings account. They can deposit a low or a high amount of money. They do this

whenever they choose. They can also

withdraw money for any purpose. The bank

will pay interest on the account balance.

However, most banks offer low interest

rates on these accounts. A better way to

TAKING A GAP YEAR TO SAVE

Students may take a gap year between high school and college. They may do this for several reasons. One reason is to work. The gap year allows students extra time to put money away for tuition. It also offers students time to think about what they want to study. A gap year gives students extra preparation time. It can even help them perform better when they get to college.

save for education is opening a college savings account.

Many college savings plans involve investments. Stocks and bonds are examples of investments. Stocks are small shares of a company. The stock value goes up when a business does well. Some stocks also pay dividends. Dividends are extra money paid to stockholders. Not all stocks have dividends. Bonds are different. They are loans made to large organizations. They can come from the government. They can also come from corporations. Bonds earn interest over time.

COLLEGE SAVINGS PLANS

One popular college savings account is a 529 plan. This account pays for college expenses. Some expenses include tuition, fees, housing, and textbooks. A 529 plan is an investment plan. It invests in stocks and bonds. It will usually earn more money than a regular savings account. People can buy stocks and bonds without a 529 plan. But they have to pay taxes on their earnings. A 529 allows the account owner to withdraw money tax-free. This is true no matter how much money the account earns. A 529 plan's benefits do not extend

Students who use money from 529 plans must be careful to spend the money only on qualifying expenses. Otherwise the money will be taxed.

to student loans. Account holders must pay taxes on money used to pay off loans. Some politicians want to change this. In 2017, bill H.R.529 was introduced. It would allow people to use 529 plans to pay off loans. As of 2019, the bill had not passed.

The company managing the 529 plan picks the stocks and bonds. Each plan has different investments. Some account owners want more say. They want to choose which companies to invest in. These people can choose a different savings plan. They may open a Coverdell Education Savings Account (ESA). This college savings plan works like a 529. But there are differences. An ESA limits how much money can be invested. It has a maximum yearly contribution of $2,000. Some people choose to open both types of accounts. They max out the Coverdell ESA.

Then they switch to the 529. A Coverdell

ESA can only be started for someone under

age eighteen. The money must be used by

age thirty.

Another savings plan is the UGMA/

UTMA plan. This stands for Uniform Gifts

or Transfers to Minors Act. This kind of

DON'T FORGET THE BOOKS

College textbooks are an expense that can add up quickly. Students can make choices that save money. Buying used textbooks is a great way to save. Renting textbooks can cost less. Some may even share textbooks with a roommate. Some colleges use OpenStax. This program publishes free or low-cost textbooks for college students. Students pay nothing for digital copies.

account does not offer tax benefits. But it has a high contribution limit. The money in these plans is not limited to tuition. It can be used for any expense. This includes student loans. When the minor turns eighteen to twenty-one, they can access the account. The age depends on what state the minor lives in.

People do not need a large deposit to start a college savings plan. Someone can open a 529 for fifteen dollars a month. The account owner can increase this amount at any time. Additional deposits can also be made at any time.

Family members can give money to 529 plans by check.

Students can also save for college

through a Roth IRA. This is a retirement

account. It offers many tax benefits. These

benefits are similar to those of college savings accounts. A Roth IRA allows students to use money for education without a **penalty**. The rest of the money stays in the plan as retirement savings.

Savings have more time to grow when people start early. But it is still worth it to open these accounts later. Any savings will reduce what students need to borrow. There are other benefits too. Having a savings plan helps students focus on getting a degree. Mark Kantrowitz is a personal finance writer. He writes, "Students who have a college savings plan

Students who are stressed about money are more likely to drop out of college.

are more likely to enroll in and graduate

from college."[7]

MANAGING THE COST

Student loans can seem like a perfect

solution. The first payment may not be

due for several years. It may seem like

Community college is a popular and affordable education option.

easy money. Miriam Caldwell writes about

personal finance. She says that later, some

people regret taking out big loans. "It

can be scary to graduate in the red with

thousands of dollars in debt," she writes.[8]

Students can make the most of their college savings by choosing a school wisely. They can save money by attending a public school. Private universities are usually more expensive. They can go to school in their home state. In-state tuition is less than out-of-state tuition. Students can also start at a community college. Community colleges usually cost less than other schools. Some students take their core courses at community colleges. They transfer to four-year universities later.

Weighing the value of a degree can also help. An expensive degree may lead to a low-paying job. This would make it harder to

pay off student loans. This does not mean

that a job needs to come with high pay

to be worthwhile. But saving money on a

degree can help people do what they love.

Many people with high student loans have

to get second jobs to make ends meet.

CONSIDER LIVING AT HOME

Students who attend an in-state college may be able to live at home. Their parents must be willing to let them stay. The cost of student housing can be expensive. It can cost as much as tuition at some universities. Students living at home save on living expenses. They can use the money for tuition. They will sacrifice some independence this way. But they may become financially independent sooner in the long run.

Many students find it helpful to get a part-time job. They may contribute money to their college savings plan. Working can also lead to practical opportunities. Some companies offer tuition reimbursement plans for employees. These plans may pay for part or all of a degree. Companies such as Chipotle, Starbucks, and Verizon offer this perk.

Savings can also come from some unexpected places. Family and friends can help. They may give to students' college savings plans. This could be instead of gifts for birthdays and holidays. Some college scholarships are even awarded as 529 contributions. This allows the scholarship money to grow.

Students can also save for college through shopping rewards programs. One example is Upromise. Rewards programs allow people to earn money through retail purchases. Some programs allow family and friends to contribute. The user shops at a store. Then a percentage of the purchase gets added to the account. Money can be transferred to a 529 plan. Students can even use money from some rewards programs to pay student loans.

Going to college can be very fulfilling. Having a financial plan can help people get there.

Paying for college is no small task. It involves a combination of scholarships, grants, loans, and savings. By being creative, students can make the most of each option. They can create the best possible plan to pay for their degrees.

WORKSHEET

To make sure others can use this book, please complete the activity on a separate sheet of paper.

CHOOSING A SCHOOL YOU CAN AFFORD

Choose three colleges and compare the costs and other details for attending each. You can find tuition prices at most schools' websites. Remember to think about room and board and other expenses, such as textbooks. After gathering this information, answer the following questions. When you are finished, rank the schools from your first to last choice.

1. What is the overall cost of tuition for this school?

2. Would this school be a good fit for what you want to study? Why?

3. Would life at this school be a good fit for you? Why?

4. What kinds of scholarships or grants might you be able to use?

5. Does the school offer work-study programs? If so, what types of work are offered?

6. Does the school help students find internships in their fields of study?

GLOSSARY

discharged

released from the responsibility to pay

diversity

the inclusion of people from a variety of races, backgrounds, religions, and other categories

economy

the wealth and resources of a community, city, or country

majors

focuses of study at a college or university

penalty

a punishment in the form of a fee

scholarship

a sum of money given to a student to pay tuition and other education costs

scouts

people sent to gather information about a person's abilities in a sport or other activity

tuition

the cost to attend a school

vocational

relating to a specific type of job, such as automotive repair or plumbing

SOURCE NOTES

CHAPTER ONE: WHY PLAN FOR COLLEGE EXPENSES?

1. Dave Ramsey, "The Best Way to Start Saving for College," *Ramsey Solutions*, n.d. www.daveramsey.com.

2. Kathryn Flynn, "Is It Ever Too Late to Start Saving for College?" *Savingforcollege.com*, November 15, 2018. www.savingforcollege.com.

CHAPTER TWO: HOW DO SCHOLARSHIPS WORK?

3. Greg Daugherty, "13 Best Tips for Winning College Scholarships," *Money*, March 28, 2016. http://money.com.

4. Kelley Holland and John W. Schoen, "Think Athletic Scholarships Are a 'Holy Grail'? Think Again," *CNBC*, October 13, 2014. www.cnbc.com

CHAPTER THREE: HOW DO GRANTS AND LOANS WORK?

5. Quoted in Teddy Nykiel, "Applying for Financial Aid for College: 6 Tips from Counselors," *NerdWallet*, March 18, 2019. www.nerdwallet.com.

6. Elizabeth Aldrich, "Federal vs. Private Student Loans: Which Should I Choose?" *The Ascent* (blog), *The Motley Fool*, March 21, 2019. www.fool.com/the-ascent.

CHAPTER FOUR: HOW CAN STUDENTS PAY FOR COLLEGE OUT OF POCKET?

7. Mark Kantrowitz, "College Savings Plans Are the Antidote to Student Loan Debt," *Forbes*, August 31, 2018. www.forbes.com.

8. Miriam Caldwell, "How to Pay for College Without Student Loans," *The Balance*, June 25, 2019. www.thebalance.com.

FOR FURTHER RESEARCH

BOOKS

Carol Christen, *What Color Is Your Parachute? For Teens*. Berkeley, CA: Ten Speed Press, 2015.

Martha London, *Saving and Investing*. San Diego, CA: ReferencePoint Press, 2020.

Carla Mooney, *Teen Guide to Paying for College*. San Diego, CA: ReferencePoint Press, 2016.

INTERNET SOURCES

Casey Bond, "Pay Off Your Student Loans Faster with These 7 Tips," *HuffPost*, January 11, 2019. www.huffpost.com.

"Finding and Applying for Scholarships," *Federal Student Aid*, n.d. https://studentaid.ed.gov.

"Which Account Is Right for Your Education Savings Goals?" *The Vanguard Group, Inc.*, n.d. https://investor.vanguard.com.

WEBSITES

Consumer Financial Protection Bureau: Paying for College

www.consumerfinance.gov/paying-for-college

The Paying for College page of the Consumer Financial Protection Bureau offers a wide variety of informative articles. Students can find information on paying for college, repaying loans, and more.

CSS Profile

https://cssprofile.collegeboard.org

The CSS Profile site is where students fill out the CSS Profile. It has guides for the process and necessary materials for the form.

FAFSA: Apply for Aid

https://studentaid.ed.gov/sa/fafsa

The FAFSA website is the portal for filling out this crucial financial aid form. It also has a variety of informative articles about many aspects of the college preparation process.

INDEX

ACT, 33
Aldrich, Elizabeth, 51
arts, 17, 33
athletes, 17, 33–35

Caldwell, Miriam, 66
Chipotle, 69
college savings accounts, 14–16, 22, 57, 58–62, 64
    Coverdell Education Savings Account (ESA), 60–61
    529 plan, 58–61, 62, 70
    Uniform Gifts or Transfers to Minors Act (UGMA/UTMA), 61–62
College Scholarship Service (CSS) Profile, 44–45
community college, 10, 67
cosign, 49
credit, 14, 47, 48–49

Daugherty, Greg, 28
deadlines, 30, 37, 39–40
debt, 14, 20, 46, 47, 49, 53, 66

Flynn, Kathryn, 22
Free Application for Federal Student Aid (FAFSA), 7, 8, 38–44

grade point average (GPA), 33
grants, 8, 15, 17, 19, 38, 40, 44, 46, 71

interest, 20, 46–48, 51, 53, 56–57
investments, 41, 57–58, 60

Kantrowitz, Mark, 64

merit, 29
military, 16

online, 27, 39

private universities, 11, 35, 44, 67

Ramsey, Dave, 14
refinance, 53
rewards programs, 70
Roth IRA, 63–64

SAT, 33
scholarships, 7, 15, 17–19, 24–37, 44, 46, 70, 71
Starbucks, 69
student aid report (SAR), 42
student loans, 8, 14, 15, 20–21, 22, 38, 46–53, 59, 62, 65, 66, 68, 70, 71
    loan forgiveness, 52, 53

textbooks, 58, 61
tuition, 7, 10–13, 17, 19, 37, 44, 56, 58, 62, 67, 68, 69

Verizon, 69

work-study programs, 19–20

IMAGE CREDITS

ABOUT THE AUTHOR

Tammy Gagne has written dozens of books for both adults and children, including *Credit Cards and Loans*. *Booklist* named her series A Teen Guide to Investing among its Top 10 Financial Series of 2013. She lives in northern New England with her husband, son, and a menagerie of pets.